AF362611

A Must Read Book
for Gifting Suppliers

10X YOUR
CORPORATE
GIFTING
BUSINESS
THROUGH SIMPLE
SOLUTIONS

KAIZAD ANKLESARIA

Worldwide Published by
Pendown Press

PENDOWN PRESS

An ISO 9001 & ISO 14001 Certified Co.,
Regd. Office: 2525/193, 1st Floor, Onkar Nagar-A,
Tri Nagar, Delhi-110035

Ph.: 09350849407, 09312235086
E-mail: info@pendownpress.com
Branch Office: 1A/2A, 20, Hari Sadan, Ansari Road,
Daryaganj, New Delhi-110002
Ph.: 011-45794768
Website: PendownPress.com

First Edition: 2022

ISBN: 978-93-5554-325-7

Layout and Cover Designed by Pendown Graphics Team
Printed and Bound in India by Thomson Press India Ltd.

Dedication

I am dedicating this book to my friends, family and team members who stood with me till the time I completed this book and spared me even when they needed me.

CONTENTS

Introduction

Who am I, and what do I do?

Hello, my name is Kaizad Anklesaria. I am into manufacturing bags, accessories and In-clinical products and am a Product Re-engineering specialist helping gifting suppliers to get their products selected in the institutions.

My tryst with bags and accessories began early in my career, nearly 15 years back. Our USP is concept development and customization as per the client's needs. This has never failed me in terms of establishing lasting relationships with my clients and also in terms of generating leads for my business.

Over the years, our concept-based products were able to help gifting suppliers generate the best ROI in our product range.

The journey so far has been brilliant.

My decision to start the business of gifting 15 years back did not prove to be very fruitful as we were not able to get good returns and repeat orders. This happened because there was no niche developed by me at that time. Hence my ROI was not good, and since it was difficult to get repeat orders from the same client, we always had to look out for new clients.

So, I decided to develop and concentrate on a niche in my product range that would help my distributors to increase their profitability.

With our 15 years of experience, deep and extensive research, and significant investment, we have developed a good solution for our gifting suppliers by penning down the problems they face and putting them in a book format that will help them.

We have been in the business of bags, accessories and clinical products for the last 15 years.

We have worked with more than 250 companies. And we have worked with all the market leaders in each industry,

We have the ability to take one single order worth 5 to 6 crore with guaranteed quality and timely delivery.

We specialize in the Pharma Industry and have worked with all major Pharma Companies.

Product managers think that I am very good at re-engineering the product as per their budget and theme, and they always rely on me. Whatever the product, I will be able to help them in creating it as per their desire.

With the tips, tools and techniques shared in this book, I assure you that you will stop losing money, 10 X, your ROI, ensure 90% conversion, bypass price undercutting from your competition and get orders worth Millions of Rupees.

If the problems listed above are not solved by your channel partner or you don't have any channel partner for this product range, you will end up losing a lot of money and will be unable to increase your product reach and increase your ROI.

 10x Your Corporate Gifting Business Through Simple Solutions

Therefore you should stop reading this book right now and check whether your channel partner is supporting you in growing or is actually holding you back and causing you to lose money.

Why this book?

I am on a mission to help the gifting companies in my product range to Ensure 90% conversion – and Increase 10X ROI:

1. **I have worked intensely** to understand the pain points of the gifting suppliers who may be startups or established suppliers and understand their needs and desires and how they operate. This helped me to come to the conclusion that if they get all the pain points solutions at one platform, it will benefit them for their growth. Through this book, I am sharing that learning.

2. **To highlight & address the problems faced by the Gifting Companies.** There are immense challenges that Gifting Companies face, as listed below, and they do not know how and where to find the solutions:

    i.   Lack of proper customized sample kits to show to their customers.

    ii. Not able to fit the product as per the theme and budget of the customer.

    iii. Undercutting the price of the product by another vendor.

    iv. Lack of Product pics with a proper shoot at one place to show the customer immediately.

    v.   Inability to quickly develop the sample.

vi. Timely Delivery, Quality checking and Packing constraints.

vii. Difficulty in finding a trusted and reliable vendor in this unorganized market.

3. **The Future of the industry is very bright but underutilized,** so I wanted that the awareness of this opportunity should be made available to a larger audience.

According to the survey of Technopak, the total market size is INR 250,000 crores for corporate gifting and personal gifting together, of which INR 12,000 Cr. belongs to the corporate gifting, which is growing over 200% per annum.

With this kind of opportunity available, the goal is to help gifting suppliers ensure 90% conversion -Increase 10 X ROI through this book.

This book addresses the mistakes and challenges Gifting Suppliers face in the industry and gives solutions for the same. This helps them increase their profitability if they work with the right channel partner.

In the following chapters, I have addressed these challenges, mistakes and myths in detail. I have shared the solutions to these and also shared valuable tips to dramatically increase conversion and enhance overall profitability.

I am sure you are excited and eager to start your journey of huge profitability, so let's deep dive without any further delay...

10x Your Corporate Gifting Business Through Simple Solutions

Acknowledgements

Before I started to write this book, all I knew was that I wanted people to know and benefit from what I've learned over these years, but then I had no clue how this was going to happen. Over time, with support from my friends, family and my team, I was able to frame this book.

I'm glad that I've been able to complete this journey without giving up.

More than anything, I'm extremely grateful to my wife Delna & my son Khushvan for being my motivation as well as my stress busters. My life and this book wouldn't be complete without their love and immense gratitude to my parents and my sister for being a wonderful family.

I am also thankful to Mr. Akshar Yadav, my mentor for his constant guidance & Mr. Dinesh Verma, CEO Pendown Press, and his team for their support and suggestions throughout the creative process.

Loss of Revenue due to Lack of Customized Sample Kit

The Challenge

90% of gifting suppliers don't have a proper customized sample kit to showcase to their customers.

Shocking!!! Isn't it??? But it's true!!!

When they go for the display, they don't have the kit, making it difficult for the product manager to select from a few samples. When the product manager asks for a particular sample, they don't have it. Hence, they have to call up different vendors for the sample in a rush.

This last-minute firefighting results in the loss of the order because of not having thc sample.

This is a very regular rule with gifting companies that they are always short of samples, and I get so many calls on a daily basis that they want samples to show to their client.

The Solution

We at Trawow give a sample kit to all our channel partners, which consists of 30 to 35 samples in the beginning and regularly update the kit with new samples.

Many of my gifting suppliers only got the order because they had the sample with them at the right time, which helped them cut the competition, convert more customers, and increase their profitability exponentially.

The Recommendation

You should always have your sample kit ready with updated new samples; hence, you are well equipped whenever there is a need to showcase to the customer.

Loss of Revenue Due To Inability To Re-Engineer The Product

The Challenge

One of the biggest challenges that blocks the revenue and progress of Gifting Companies is they are unable to fit the product as per the theme and budget of the customer.

The problem is when the company approves of a certain product and then asks for the product to be designed at a specific budget. However, the majority of the Gifting Companies don't have a strong channel partner who has the expertise to Re-engineer the product; hence they are stuck at that time.

They lose the order as they cannot provide a proper and effective solution to the customer to create a balance between their choice and their budget.

The Solution

We have specialized in this business for the last 15 years and have an in-house sampling facility that helps design and re-engineer the product as per the budget and theme.

We have developed the ability and skills to re-engineer the product as per theme and budget every day and ensure that our clients don't ever lose the order.

The Recommendation

Gifting suppliers should have channel partners who are experts in that category of product. These expert channel partners will support them in designing and fitting the product as per the customer's budget on a continuous basis.

10x Your Corporate Gifting Business Through Simple Solutions

Loss of Revenue due to Price-Undercutting by the Competition

The Challenge

Perhaps the most critical challenge the Gifting Companies face is the undercutting of the product price by another vendor.

The challenges the Gifting Company faces is they are not able to be the differentiator of the product and make the classic mistake of offering products that are commonly available in the market. There is no USP in the product, and it is easy to copy; hence the other vendors are able to undercut the price and bag the order [even though they may be offering a product that is lower in quality].

The Solution

To be the differentiator, we give properly customized products that are not readily available, and the materials used are very specific and unique. This ensures that there is almost zero competition from the market.

The Recommendation

It is advisable and assuredly profitable to work with channel partners who can help in developing products that are not common but are unique and have USPs in their product range. This will ensure more than 90% conversion.

10x Your Corporate Gifting Business Through Simple Solutions

Loss of Revenue due to Lack of proper Product Shoots & Gallery

The Challenge

Another challenge that leads to loss of revenue for Gifting Companies is the unavailability of product pictures with a proper shoot at all stored in one place to show to their customers immediately.

Gifting companies deal in a lot of different categories of products. It is difficult for them to have a proper product shot for each category in one place.

As a result, they are always fire fighting for the picture at the last moment when the customers ask for it and waste a lot of time and energy trying to find it.

Sometimes they cannot find the picture where they have stored it and are unable to provide prompt service to the customer resulting in the loss of the order just by not having the right picture at the right time.

The Solution

To help the customer, we have developed a WhatsApp Bot for pictures of each and every product.

It is completely automated where you can view pictures price-wise, product-wise and budget-wise for each and every product category.

This Bot is uploaded on a regular basis, and when a new product is developed, a proper shoot is done, and its product shots are added to the Bot.

You can download anything from the Bot within seconds, and customers can view the product pictures any time, 24x7. All the products are professionally shot, which helps the customers to visualize them better.

The Recommendation

Gifting Companies should have a picture of all the products in one place, which should be used as the marketing kit collateral to help them get orders. The first point of customer interaction is the picture of the product, and if you don't have a proper picture, you will not be able to service them properly and will lose the order.

Loss of Revenue Due To Inability To Develop Sample Fast

The Challenge

Another key challenge Gifting Companies face is not being able to develop the sample fast when required.

Even though the Gifting Company has the sample and likes it, there are always minor changes and adjustments to be made in the sample as per the client's needs. This means that the Gifting Companies have to develop the new sample in the fastest time possible and give it to the customer. Since most of the time they don't have a reliable channel partner, they are not able to produce the correct sample fast, and generally, there is a delay. This delay can prove to be fatal and lead to a loss of an order that was literally theirs for the taking.

The Solution

We provide immediate solutions as we have dedicated, specialized sample makers sitting right in our office. These highly specialized and experienced sample makers help develop the sample at the earliest and help you modify and change it several times as per the need of the customer.

The Recommendation

Just having the sample will not solve the problem; if you don't have proper backup support, you will not be able to service the client and will lose the order because of not servicing the client on time. Clients are very demanding, and they want everything immediately. So, it is essential to have a channel partner who can develop and modify samples speedily and service the client promptly.

❖ ❖ ❖

Increased Burden of Costs Due To Delayed Timelines

The Problem

A major problem plaguing the Gifting Companies is that the delivery timelines are not maintained. This increases the cost and time of the Gifting Company.

A majority of the Gifting Suppliers are sourcing products from unorganized players where they have to do a lot of follow up in order to maintain the timelines.

They have to do a lot of chik-chik [unnecessary stressful interaction] with the vendor. They waste a lot of time on the vendor following up for the delivery as there is a very high penalty clause if the material is not supplied on time.

This results in a significant loss in revenue and time invested with absolutely no return.

The Solution

We have a proper in-house autopilot system that allows us to track the production regularly. And we communicate with our customers daily hence they know the progress of the supplies.

Due to these stringent measures and proper planning, scheduling and tracking, 99% of our deliveries are on time. And if ever there is a genuine delay from our side, we will bear the penalty, which other unorganized players are not able to do.

The Recommendation

You are advised to work with an organized channel partner having a good track record of timely delivery, which will help to save your energy and cost.

Loss Due To QC & Packing Being Assigned To Unskilled Staff

The Mistake

A big mistake Gifting Companies make without realizing the dire consequences is getting the product quality check and packing done by unskilled people and not professionally qualified staff.

Due to a price constraint, Gifting Companies make the mistake of getting their local unorganized vendor to do the QC and pack the goods.

Chances are, the material is not checked properly as their intention is good, but they are not experts in checking, which leads to penalties and other problems once the goods are delivered.

Sometimes the packing is not properly done in terms of labeling and quantity not matching, leading to a high penalty.

Even if one bag is missing in one carton, the penalty can be as high as 20000/ Rs in some companies.

The Solution

We have a proper 6000 sq feet warehouse at Bhiwandi, where professional checking and packing is done. There are proper systems laid down for the QC and packing such that the chances of error are negligible.

This helps our channel partners to rely on us completely and have peace of mind and save their costs by way of penalty.

The Recommendation

Never rely on the local unorganized players for the checking and packing of the product. This will cost you a high penalty, and you will not end up saving money as you had thought but will end up paying much more.

 10x Your Corporate Gifting Business Through Simple Solutions

8

Loss Due To Not Mapping Your Audience

The Mistake

Not Mapping your audience.

Gifting Companies make the mistake of not focusing on each and every product manager and checking on what they require in all the 4 quarters as per their budget and theme. They just randomly respond as and when the product managers raise the need. Hence, they miss out on the opportunity to generate more leads and conversions right at the beginning of the year.

There are product managers who need inputs 4 times a year. Suppose a product manager wants to do the input 4 times a year, but you have not mapped them properly from their database as to who wants what type of product and their budget 4 times a year. You miss out on a great opportunity.

The Solution

Requirements of each product manager should be known in advance, and a PPT to be ready for each product manager as per their requirement and in their brand.

If proper Mapping is done, the order can be closed for all 4 quarters right at the beginning of the year.

The Tip

Gifting companies should ensure that they review their DATABASE of product managers and map each and every product manager to identify their product requirement and budget for all the 4 quarters backed by a customized PPT at the beginning of the year.

Based on the Mapping and customized PPTs they should then approach them at the beginning of the year and cash on the opportunity of closing the order for the entire year.

 10x Your Corporate Gifting Business Through Simple Solutions

Loss Due To Not Focusing On Regular, High Ticket Products

The Mistake

Not focusing on the category of Bags, Accessories and In-clinical products which can give maximum returns.

Gifting Suppliers often make the mistake of trying to work with very high branded companies for this category. So, they are not able to service the needs of the product manager who wants a budget product with customization.

They are not able to trust vendors in this category as this is a very unorganized market, and many gifting suppliers have burnt their fingers; hence they try to avoid this category and lose business.

The Solution

These products are utility products where 90% of our products are in the range of 75 Rs. to 375 Rs. There is a lot of customization possible by way of budget and theme in these products and can be used as the continuity theme. If marketed properly, this range of products can get you orders in all 4 quarters.

As per the International Gifting Matrix, these products are the best gifting options fitting all the criteria of the Matrix checklist, as listed below

1. Is there a continuity theme?

2. Is it practical?

3. Is it visible?

4. Can it be personalized?

5. Can it be customized?

The Recommendation

Bags, accessories and In-clinical products are essentials to be kept in the portfolio. As the requirements of these products are on a regular basis and orders in this category are high ticket orders. This category provides you with the best ROI.

Loss Due To The Gifting Company Trying To Do Everything By Them Self

The Mistake

Gifting Companies trying to do everything by themselves.

Most of the Gifting Suppliers want to earn maximum profit and personally try to do everything, from production to sourcing to packing to delivery which sucks their energy and time majorly.

This may result in profits in the particular order, but this prevents them from scaling up and earning more profits overall as they have less time to focus on strategizing and marketing because they are too involved in the day to day operational work.

The Solution

The Gifting Company should try to outsource most of the functions to a reliable vendor who can help them serve everything and give end-to-end solutions like checking, packing and delivery of the product.

Overall, this will help save money on transportation, rent of godown and packing costs. This will also leave you free to focus on marketing and business development activities which will generate more orders.

The Recommendation

Never try to do everything yourself. Instead, identify and work with a proper channel partner who can provide you with end-to-end solutions, leaving you free to concentrate on building your business and market.

 10x Your Corporate Gifting Business Through Simple Solutions

Loss Due to Buying The Product at a Cheaper Price from Unorganized Players

The Myth

Buying the product from the unorganized partner at a cheaper price will increase profitability.

If you are working with an unorganized channel partner, I ask you one simple question? How many times will you be able to copy the product and get your order converted? It can be done one, two or three times but not every time.

Unorganized players copy the product and give you the product at a cheaper cost but do not add value every time. Gifting Companies should go deep into it and check out what other value addition the vendor can offer which will be beneficial for their growth.

Gifting companies waste a lot of energy doing chik-chik with the unorganized vendor. They waste a lot of time on the vendor, which in turn leads to less time for marketing activities and consequently lesser profits.

The Solution

It is a myth that buying from organized channel partners is expensive.

Organized channel partners will help you get orders continuously by providing value-added services like fast sampling, new samples at regular intervals, and developing concept-based products to get the order.

Organized players give end-to-end solutions that can help check, pack, and deliver the product and provide products with high perceived value, leading to higher and faster conversions.

The Recommendation

Working with organized players can help you grow your business and benefit you by doing more orders with them. This will help build a stable working partnership that leads to smoother functioning, higher conversions and on-time delivery that will help you have an excellent reputation in the market.

On the other hand, if you work with unorganized players, you will be able to do just one or two orders with them temporarily as they will not be able to fulfill your expectations leading to loss of orders and reputation. And then you will have to search for a partner all over again, leading to a loss of time and money.

❖ ❖ ❖

To Recap in a Nutshell

1. 90% of Gifting Suppliers don't have a proper customized sample kit to showcase to their customers.

2. Most Gifting Companies are not able to fit the product as per the theme and budget of the customer.

3. Most Gifting Companies are plagued by price undercutting of the product by another vendor.

4. Gifting Companies do not have properly shot product pictures available at one place to be shown to customers immediately.

5. Gifting Companies are not able to develop the sample fast when required leading to loss of orders.

6. Delivery timelines not being maintained increases the cost and time of the Gifting Companies leading to loss of revenue.

7. Gifting Companies make the mistake of getting the product quality check and packing done by local inexperienced people instead of professionally trained and experienced staff.

8. Gifting Companies make the mistake of not Mapping their audience, missing out on opportunities to close big orders with ease right at the beginning of the year for all 4 quarters.

9. Gifting Companies make the mistake of not focusing on the category of Bags, Accessories and In-clinical products, which can give maximum returns.

10. Gifting Companies try to do everything by themselves to save costs but actually end up losing money.

11. Gifting Companies believe in the MYTH that buying the product from the unorganized partner at a cheaper price will increase profitability.

10x Your Corporate Gifting Business Through Simple Solutions

Let's Continue
The Journey to Profitability...

Thank you for reading this book. That you have made it to this page tells me that you are genuinely interested in taking your Gifting Business to the next level and are willing to work on it. If you follow the solutions and tips shared in this book, I assure you that you will be able to enhance conversions and profits significantly and get the lion's share of the market.

Let this not be the end of our journey together. I can be a part of your phenomenal growth journey.

My expertise is available to support you and help you take your gifting business to the next level.

Wishing you the "Gift of Success & Profitability."

Your partner in success

Kaizad Anklesaria

Reach out or connect with me at:

- 📞 +91 98208 07547
- 🟢 +91 99670 78398
- ✉️ www.gmail.com/kaizadanklesaria22@gmail.com
- 💼 Linkedin.com/Kaizad Anklesaria
- 📘 www.facebook.com/Trawow Bags
- 📷 www.instagram.com/Trawowbags

❖ ❖ ❖

10x Your Corporate Gifting Business Through Simple Solutions

The Truth Tells Its Own Story!

Testimonials From Esteemed Clients

I have known Kaizad for the last 10 years and he can give an efficient end-to-end solution and has an amazing ability for Re-Engineering the product right from designing the product, manufacturing the same with customized packaging, and delivering the products directly to the customers with timely delivery and quality. They can do the required sampling at the earliest, which helps us to close the order at the earliest and hence can generate more profitable business. It is always profitable to work with a channel partner like Kaizad.

Pankaj Jain Director
KKCL Keval Kiran clothing ltd
(Killer, Easies, LawmanPg3, Integriti and Desibelle)

Kaizad from Trawow has an amazing ability to Re-Engineer products at a very competitive price, with a high perceived value. We have high volume requirements as we sell our products online pan India. We sometimes sell 10,000 combo bags in a single day, and Trawow is the solution, every time with their timely delivery and quality.

Naaptol
Moeez Khan, Senior Category manager
(No 1 Home shop Indian Company)

As we had to launch a product within a very short time, we needed fast and timely delivery. Trawow, with their fantastic TAT, was our solution and face-saver. Recently, we needed 5,000 Duffel suit cover bags within one month. They did it well within time without compromising on the quality. Kudos to them.

Arvind Ltd

Raunaq Sharma, Vice President marketing

We have been associated with Trawow for a long time. Their USP is the wide spectrum of choices on offer at various price points. For us, Kaizad from Trawow is the top-of-the-mind brand. They are the one-stop destination for a variety of solutions without compromising on quality and delivery.

Hindustan Petroleum Corporation (HPCL)

Anupam Tiwari, GM Corporate Affairs and Official Language

We have been associated with Trawow for a long time. We always use their bags for our sales team, which they use all throughout the year. Despite rough use by salespeople, the quality is maintained.

Empire Spices & Foods Ltd

Hemant Gaurkar, Purchase Manager

Trawow can give an efficient end-to-end solution. Their efficiency is visible right from designing the product, manufacturing the same with customized packaging, and delivering the products to the customers, spread across India through their courier partners. They have delivered nearly 18000 bags in the past one year and did it well without compromising on quality.

Ratnakar Bank Ltd (RBL)

Karik Ambe

Kaizad from Trawow has an amazing ability to Re-Engineer our customized packaging for our beauty products at a very competitive price, with a high perceived value and very attractive looks. Whenever there is a requirement for customized packaging, he is our only choice for all our pouches and small bags for the packaging of the beauty products.

SSIZ international

Purvi Shah, Business Head-SSIZ international

Being their long tenure happy customer, I am delighted to share my experience with Trawow.

A wide range of product lines and refined quality is their foundation for building customer delight. Along with their personalization, their customizing option also gives you the liberty to explore and add your feelings through every purchase you make for your customers and helps you build upon your campaigns.

Sun Pharma Laboratories Ltd

Konark Dinkar-Group Product Manager

Trawow has the ability to Re-Engineer products at a very competitive price yet with a high perceived value. Whenever there is a requirement for bags and accessories or in-clinical products, we think of Trawow. Trawow is the solution, every time.

Vivan life Science

Dipti Jain, Director

We have been associated with Trawow for a long time. For us, Trawow is the top-of-the-mind brand. They are the one-stop destination for a variety of solutions without compromising on delivery.

Manipal Cigna Health Insurance
Mukesh Shetty, Sales Strategy

Trawow can give an efficient end-to-end solution. Their efficiency is visible from designing the product, manufacturing the same with customized packaging, and delivering the products to the customers, spread across India through their courier partners.

British Deputy High Commission
Navaz Antia, Consular officer Western India

Whenever there is a requirement for bags and accessories or in-clinical products, we think of them. Trawow is the solution, every time.

IPCA Laboratories Ltd
Simantinee Panja

We have been associated with Trawow for a long time. For us, Kaizad from Trawow is the top-of-the-mind brand. They are the one-stop destination offering multiple solutions without compromising quality and delivery.

Yash Pharma Laboratories Pvt Ltd
Dinesh Mhatre, Manager HR & Admin

These prestigious logos of the market leaders that are our delighted customers are the greatest testimonials to the excellence of our products/services.

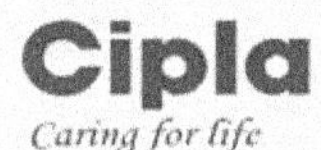